WITHDRAWN

BROTHERS,
I LOVED YOU ALL

(Poems, 1969-1977)

by Hayden Carruth

The Sheep Meadow Press
New York City

ACKNOWLEDGMENTS

These poems have been previously published in: *American Poetry Review, Bleb, Caterpillar, The Cat and the Moon, Esquire, The Georgia Review, Hearse, The Hudson Review, Kayak, The Lamp in the Spine, The Massachusetts Review, The Nation, New Letters, The New Yorker, The Ohio Review, The Ontario Review, Poetry Northwest, Poetry Now, The Salt Creek Reader, The Sewanee Review, The Southern Review, The Texas Quarterly, The Virginia Quarterly Review.*

"Aura" has been published in a limited edition by The Janus Press. "Paragraphs" has been published in a limited edition by The Crow's Mark Press.

I owe thanks also to the National Endowment for the Arts, the Mark Rothko Foundation, the Ariadne Foundation, and the Vermont Council on the Arts for grants of financial assistance during the years when these poems were written. And I am especially grateful to John Engels, Geof Hewitt, Galway Kinnell, and Sue Standing for help during the preparation of the book.

ISBN 0-8180-1543-8 (cloth); 0-8180-1544-6 (paper)
Library of Congress Catalog Card Number 77-95138
First printing

for Marshall

Contents

The Loon on Forrester's Pond

Summer wilderness, a blue light
twinkling in trees and water, but even
wilderness is deprived now. "What's that?
What is that sound?" Then it came to me,
this insane song, wavering music
like the cry of the genie inside the lamp,
it came from inside the long wilderness
of my life, a loon's song, and there he was
swimming on the pond, guarding
his mate's nest by the shore,
diving and staying under
unbelievable minutes and coming up
where no one was looking. My friend
told how once in his boyhood
he had seen a loon swimming beneath his boat,
a shape dark and powerful
down in that silent world, and how
it had ejected a plume of white excrement
curving behind. "It was beautiful,"
he said.

The loon
broke the stillness over the water
again and again,

broke the wilderness
with his song, truly
a vestige, the laugh that transcends
first all mirth
and then all sorrow
and finally all knowledge, dying
into the gentlest quavering timeless
woe. It seemed
the real and only sanity to me.

When Howitzers Began

When howitzers began
   the fish darted downward
to weeds and rocks,
   dark forms motionless
in darkness, yet they were
   stunned and again
stunned
   and again and
again stunned, until their
   lives loosened, spreading
a darker darkness
   over the river.

August First

Late night on the porch, thinking
of old poems. Another day's
work, another evening's,
done. A large moth, probably
Catocala, batters the screen,
but lazily, its strength spent,
its wings tattered. It perches
trembling on the sill. The sky
is hot dark summer, neither
moon nor stars, air unstirring,
darkness complete; and the brook
sounds low, a discourse fumbling
among obstinate stones. I
remember a poem I wrote
years ago when my wife and
I had been married twenty-
two days, an exuberant
poem of love, death, the white
snow, personal purity. Now
I look without seeing at
a geranium on the sill;
and, still full of day and evening,
of what to do for money,
I wonder what became of
purity. The world is a
complex fatigue. The moth tries
once more, wavering desperately
up the screen, beating, insane,
behind the geranium. It
is an immense geranium,
the biggest I've ever seen,

with a stem like a small tree
branching, so that two thick arms
rise against the blackness of
this summer sky, and hold up
ten blossom clusters, bright bursts
of color. What is it — coral,
mallow? Isn't there a color
called "geranium"? No matter.
They are clusters of richness
held against the night in quiet
exultation, five on each branch,
upraised. I bought it myself
and gave it to my young wife
years ago, a plastic cup
with a 19¢ seedling
from the supermarket, now
so thick, leathery-stemmed,
and bountiful with blossom.
The moth rests again, clinging.
The brook talks. The night listens.

That I Had Had Courage When Young

Yet had I not much
who went out — out! — among those
heartless all around, to look
and talk sometimes and touch?

In the big lunatic house
I did not fly apart nor spatter
the walls with myself, not quite.
I sat with madness in my mouth.

But never, it was never enough.
Else how could all these books
I did not write bend down my back
grown now so old and tough?

Essay

So many poems about the deaths of animals.
Wilbur's toad, Kinnell's porcupine, Eberhart's squirrel,
and that poem by someone — Hecht? Merrill? —
about cremating a woodchuck. But mostly
I remember the outrageous number of them,
as if *every* poet, I too, had written at least
one animal elegy; with the result that today
when I came to a good enough poem by Edwin Brock
about finding a dead fox at the edge of the sea
I could not respond; as if permanent shock
had deadened me. And then after a moment
I began to give way to sorrow (watching myself
sorrowlessly the while), not merely because
part of my being had been violated and annulled,
but because all these many poems over the years
have been necessary, — suitable and correct. This
has been the time of the finishing off of the animals.
They are going away — their fur and their wild eyes,
their voices. Deer leap and leap in front
of the screaming snowmobiles until they leap
out of existence. Hawks circle once or twice
around their shattered nests and then they climb
to the stars. I have lived with them fifty years,
we have lived with them fifty million years,
and now they are going, almost gone. I don't know
if the animals are capable of reproach.
But clearly they do not bother to say good-bye.

The Joy and Agony of Improvisation

There, the moon, just appearing
over dark pines, heavy and round,
the color of old parchment; and indeed
it seems archaic. What does it mean
in our histories, yours and mine,
except a myth no longer altogether
necessary, a theorem proven in another
millennium? This is a peculiar night,
uncomfortable. Well, it is like most moments
of the present, it doesn't fit us.
The low night wind, shifting, directionless,
moves the pine boughs, as if — so you say —
we were in the midst of voices in some
obscure contention. Of course we are.
But not obscure, only fruitless, stupid,
and very dangerous. Come,
let's go in the tent and sleep.

Later

we waken, knowing the night has changed.
It's a high wind now. Strange how the voices
have turned to song. Hear
it rising, rising, then breaking, then
rising again, and breaking again. Oh, something
is unutterable, the song cannot reach it.
Yet we know it, know what we cannot
hear — out on the night's great circle,
the circle of consciousness with its far rim always
hidden, there where suffering and joy
meet and combine,
the inexpressible. How the song is striving

and how beautifully failing — the measure
of beauty, beyond plenitude,
never but always enough. Come
outside again, under tossing pines
and the racing clouds. This
is more than we could ever have meant
in our kiss; it is the gathering of our love
into all love, into that suffering and joy.
And see, up there in the sky, uncovered now
as the clouds stream away,
the moon,
so new, so clean and high and bright and true.

For Denise and Mitch

The oven door creaks
in the night in the silent
house, like all old things.
I rap the loaves, top
and bottom, and return them
for ten minutes more.
                    I wish
you could come through the door
out of the dark and snow. I wish
you two could come without words,
no exclamations, nothing
to betray the time, the distance
between us, but as if
what's happening in my chest
were no pain, nor the spreading
stain on the backs of my hands
an actual turning. We are
ourselves, aren't we? — presences
in the smell of new bread
here, now, always.
The house creaks in the cold,
the planet creaks, turning
beneath old stars, and we —
we listen without words,
smiling to one another.
                    I'll eat
the first cut of the warm loaf,
brown as the backs of my hands,
for you.

My Hut

(after Tran Quang Khai)

Built long ago, old
sills rotting in mud,
filled now with soft ash
from a thousand fires that warmed me,
ash settled indelibly
on these books, never
to be clean again,
and on these shoulders
and hands.

In Memoriam

This warmish night of the thaw
in January a beech chunk
smoldering in my Herald
No. 22A box stove suddenly
takes fire and burns
hot, or rather I suddenly
who was reading the sweet
and bitter poems of Paul
Goodman dead last summer
am aware how my shed
becomes a furnace, and taking
my shovel I ladle
a great mush of snow
into the stove's mouth
to quieten it
and then step quickly
outside again to watch
the plume of steam rise
from my stovepipe straightly
and vanish into the mist.

Mending the Adobe

Sun dazzle and black shadow,
crow caw and magpie rattle
where I saw a pueblo woman,
dark and small, who stood
on a ponderosa block
outside her home to smear
rich mud on the wall, red
and oily mud, using her
hands and a thin wooden
paddle. It shone smoothly,
and she left a swirling
pattern that I liked, although
I looked and said nothing.
When she stepped down for more
mud she said, "Sometimes
I fix it, sometimes not.
Mostly I fix it — now
in the dry time before rain.
That's good. But sometimes
I say the hell with it,
the rain will only wash it,
the frost crack it, the wind
blow it away. I'm not so
young no more. Well, but mostly
I fix it, I feel better
when I fix it — you know?
I remember my mother."

The Little Fire in the Woods

Even these stones I placed crudely once,
black now from many fires, bring me
a little knowledge, things I've done,
times endured, saying I am this one, this
person, as night falls through the trees. I see sand
darkening by the edge of an ocean, lights
on the rim of a galaxy, but I have not planned

my visions. I wish I could. We used birch bark
and spruce cones for tinder tonight, in which
a spark rambled until it met itself, flaring then
and leaping, throwing shadows among the trees.
Now punky gray birch smolders. Held
In the roots of our great spruce, I hold
my son, and the darkness thickens. It isn't

the cares of day I think of any longer.
True, I got this bruised belly when the machine
kicked this afternoon in our troubled potato patch
where the earth too cried out for justice,
justice! I tauten my muscles; the pain
is good and I wish it could be everything. But
larger errors are what we think of now

that have flared and leapt and thrown these shadows
of extinction among our objects. Or is the error
necessity, a circle closing? Son, in nature all
successions end. How long and slow is chaos.
Anywhere I am I see the slow surge of fire —
I, a diffraction, nothing. My son moves
closer. ''Pop, how does the fire make heat?''

He does not see the fire I see, but I know
he knows a terror that children have never
known before, waiting for him. He knows.
Our love is here, this night, these woods, existing;
it is now. I think how its being
must emanate, like heat in conversion,
out beyond the woods to the stars, and how

it joins there in the total reckoning. It *must*.
Could anyone resist this longing all the time?
Oh, I know what I know, and I cannot
unknow it, crying out too for justice,
while the fire dwindles and shadows rise and flow.
But listen, something is here in the forest. Listen.
It is very clear and it whispers a little song:

> Sweet Bo I know thee
> > > thou art ten
> and knowest now thy father is
> five times more again
> > > and more
> and most gone out of rhymes
> sweet Bo
> > > for thou dost know me

> And thou old spruce above us
> many are they of comrade and kin
> who love us
> > > so that their loving proveth
> everything
> > > although their way hath not
> the same compassion
> > > as thy nonloving.

Sweet Bo good night and hold me
hold me close
              the good firelight
is dying
       the woods are sighing
and great is the dark
                 grateful
am I for thee sweet Bo
                good night
good night.

The Mountain Cabin

Hour by hour the storm deepened. He read,
not much, less than most days, and watched

the wind driving the snow in its circle,
mountain to mountain, forty miles around.

He was o.k., nothing wrong. But he knew
— and knew he could not stop knowing —

he was trapped, couldn't go down, would lose
his trail in storm, the red-gashed blazes

blown out. He'd end in the lowland thickets,
frozen. Today what he had chosen

had chosen him. He tended the stove,
refilled the kettle with snow, drank tea, watched

blue smoke from his stovepipe twist downward
with writhing swiftness into the trees,

recounted his cigars, shuffled the letters
he'd brought to answer. Whiteness

trickled under the door, hoarfrost grew
on the nailheads. He tested the harness

of his snowshoes, cold greased leather.
At sunset unexpected color-of-pewter

shone for five minutes in the western notch.
Then he lit the lamp. It flickered, teased

by the wind hunting through the walls,
so that the glass blackened and the flame,

without shrinking, became remote, an orange
specter. He listened. Now at night

the storm seemed unrelated, an absolute,
the unseen whole of otherness out there.

His light was a dusky ovoid floating
at the top of the lamp on darkness.

In time he got up, stiff and cold,
and leaned over the lamp and blew it out.

Family Reunion

Gathered at the time of thanks; and the harvest
is gathered in, and earth and sky are cold,
the standing weeds are brown; and the lady

of the house is tremblingly brown and old
who had once grown like a flower, and the third son,
in his rich suit as soft as summer, smiles

his dear smile, and smiles and smiles, till it fades
to the haggard smile of freezing and pallor
and deep hidden pain, and the second son

moves heavily and laughs heavily, the gray
specter of the lady's husband who is dead,
and the first son who has come the longest way

smiles awkwardly in a head gone out of true
and made of fearful crookedness, and he wonders
what harvest, what harvest now; and the children

are forgotten upstairs in God knows what old games,
and the wives recede adroitly to another room,
and the dog walks among the smiles, sniffs them

for their aroma of things found in the field
and rolls in them; and later, when all is done,
the first son sits under the family clock on the mantel

that is older than them all, and he looks in the dark
window to see whose face is there, and the clock
walks in its place, a dreadful steady tread,

step, step, step, where it was always walked,
and the first son looks at the ashtrays, the glasses
redolent of ceremonial whisky and wine,

the chairs out of their places, and the lines of his head
plot strange diagrams on the window; and thanks,
he says, thanks, thanks, not said but shouted

in the outcry of hours, protesting stars and the moon,
and the sleepless clock says it too, thanks once,
thanks twice, thanks three o'clock, and the man,

who is the sleepless first son from farthest away,
says thanks, thanks again, thanks just the same.
What more could he, what more would you have him, say?

The Mountain

Black summer, black Vermont. Who sees
this mountain rising nearby
in the darkness? But we

know it there. On the other side
in a black street of a black city
a man who is probably black

carries a Thompson
submachinegun, and don't
tell me how that feels

who carried one two years
in Italy; blunt-barreled power,
smooth simple unfailing mechanism

— the only gun whose recoil
tugs you forward, toward
the target, almost

like love. Separated
by this immense hill we share nevertheless
a certain knowledge of tactics

and a common attitude toward reality.
Flickering neon, like moonlight in beech leaves,
is fine camouflage. To destroy

can be beautiful.
I remember Mussolini's
bombed statues by the *dopolavoro* pavilion,

thick monsters transformed to elegance
by their broken heads and cut-off
arms. Let the city be transformed.

A man with a submachinegun is
invulnerable, the sniper's
sharp little steel or the fist

of a grenade always
finds him surprised. Hey,
look out, man! What you

trying to do, get yourself
killed? They're everywhere, everywhere,
hear? — the night's

full of them and they're looking
for a dead nigger — so watch it,
and go on fox feet and listen like a bat;

remember everything I told you.
You got to be smart enough
for both of us now.

But are you there? Are you
really there?

Essay on Stone

April abomination, that's what I call
this wet snow sneaking down day after day,
    down the edges of air, when we
      were primed for spring.

The flowers of May will come next week — in theory.
And I suppose that witty sentimentalist,
    Heine, saw this same snow falling
      in the North Sea

as into the Abyss. I look out now across
this pasture, the mud and wet matted grass,
    the waving billows of it, where
      the snow is falling

as into our own abyss. I stand on Marshall's
great rock, to which I have returned, fascinated,
    a thousand times, I stand as if
      on a headland

or on an islet in the midst of waves,
and what is this fascination, this cold desire?
    Once I wrote a poem about
      making love to stone

and a whole book in which the protagonist,
who was myself, carried a stone with him
    everywhere he went. I still like
      that poem and that book,

and yet for all my years of stone-loving
I've learned not much about stone. Oh,
          I can tell slate from quartz from sandstone —
               who couldn't? — and here

in this district we even have an exotic
stone, the talc, that feels warm and bloody
          in one's hand, but basically I am
               ignorant. Let

the geologists keep their igneous pyrites
to themselves. I don't even know if
          this great rock, projecting
               bigger than a barn

from the slope of the pasture, is a free
boulder that may have come here from the top
          of Butternut Mountain who knows
               how many eons ago,

or part of the underlying granite of Vermont.
I stand on its back, looking into the abyss.
          At all events the fascination
               is undeniable. I

always said there could be no absolutes,
but this is stone, stone, stone —
          so here, so perfectly
               here. It is

the abyss inverted, the abyss made visible.
Years ago when I wrote that other poem
    I might have taken pleasure from this,
        I think I would have. Now

I am fifty-three going on fifty-four,
a rotten time of life. My end-of-winter clothes
    are threadbare, my boots cracked, and how
        astonishing to see

my back, like that figure in Rembrandt's drawing,
bent. I shift weight on my walking-stick
    and the stick slips in wet lichen
        and then my boots skid too,

and down I go — not hurt, just shaken.
And what a hurt that is! Is it consoling
    to know I might have fallen
        into the abyss?

All this in silence, every word of it spoken
in my mind. The snow falls. Heine,
    there must be something wrong with us.
        I've heard this pasture

moaning at my feet for years, as you heard
that gray sea, we two shaken and always
    unconsoled by what we love,
        the absolute stone.

After the Winter of Many Thaws

March is murder. In nature
rebirth will follow, we know, an upheaval
greater than death, but sometimes it
doesn't matter. We slip, wallow
in sucking greasy snow, and the blackbird
that came four days ago
cries on his fencepost in hunger. Fingers
of ice cling to the ledges. A gravid doe,
floundering, unable to run,
looks at us with weariness and starvation
in her eyes, pathos
older, deeper, and terribly more direct
than any in men's eyes. Then
we see the great rock altered,
the rock brought here
thousands and thousands of years ago,
changed now, its covering
that had lain over it perhaps for centuries
now in one winter of unaccustomed weather
fallen away — moss, the red soldier lichen,
ground pine, fern, partridgeberry, and a white
birch sapling rooted there
bright and pristine, now all fallen, gone
to brown rubble in snow at the foot
of the great rock. It had been a kind of garden
whose variegation we had studied in many seasons,
now pale gray, veined, and strangely clean. This thing
was done by the machine of the stars,
their mindless wind and sun and rain — but ''done''
in no sense I know. I thought then
of words I had sometimes made to brighten

with what I took for meaning. But this light
was the granite-light that comes
from under earth, spectral, pale gray,
light dense and with no clarity
and more obscure than shadow. And I remembered
my first sight of it
(for it comes from anywhere, or everywhere),
how snow had fallen
years past, gray light fragmented from above
that I had looked at with curiosity
on my sleeve and had seen nothing, and when
the human glass showed me crystals
I had seen nothing magnified. We turned away again,
homeward through heavy drifts, helping one another,
arms, shoulders, hips for leverage,
silent for the essential beauty whose terror
can never be uttered. Nothing has been done
and always will be done. Beauty
is the lightless light that is
the silence that is
the stone
in the eye of the world forever.

Valentine

That you should still send
yourself to me, that you should
arrive and attend like this
when there is no reason, when
actually there may be

contrary reasons, remains
the one phenomenon to me
most wonderful. Please,
lie back a moment, raise
your arm. I love to see

how the heart buries its
point in your groin, so dearly,
though it would be nothing
without its upward rounding
and flectioning over your

belly. Don't you believe
what you've been told, that now
valentines are grievous, all
the more for those as old
as we are? Still you come,

still you present this heart
with its swelling curves.
In wintertime I work
all night for quiet and then
go out to watch the dawn,

how February's bright stars
fade so that only knowing —
the mind — can tell they're there.
Strange that the light should be
a concealment. Yet I think

that's how it is with us, we
who are "enlightened," who know
sex and the hurt of sex,
yes, the era's learning, so
necessary. But still the older

and farther, farthest lights
shine behind the day, there
for our minds, or something
in us, to remember. Sweetly,
smilingly, when I come in

you throw the covers back,
an unconcealment, sending
from sleep your valentine
in the light the windows shed,
ice-laced, on your warm bed.

Once and Again

The peace of green summer lay over this meadow so
       deeply once
that I thought of England, cows lazy on the sward, the
       great elm
rising above them in diaphanous arches, the meadow
       that Marvell might have seen
from his study window but that I have never seen, yet I
       saw it
here. It *was* here, but that so long ago. And now the elms
of this region have mostly died, it is mid-November, the
       gray season,
purple on wooded hills, the meadow is gray and bare, the
       cows
are in their barn. I thought of England because so many
       things I love
have come from England, many images in my memory,
       although
I have never been there and have little hope that I will
       ever go.
I stand in the grayness, searching, looking for something
       without knowing what,
until I remember the great elm that used to be. To
       believe in the God
who does not exist is a heroism of faith, much needed in
       these times,
I agree, I know, especially since the hero is and must
       always be
unrecognized. But to love the God that does not exist, to
       love the love

that does not exist, this is more than heroism, it is
      perhaps almost
saintliness, such as we can know it. To discover and to
      hold, to resurrect
an idea for its own sake. Ah my heart, how you quicken in
      unrecognized energy
as hard little pellets of snow come stinging, driven on the
      gray wind.

November Jeans Song

Hey, hey, daddio,
Them old jeans is
   Going to go!

Rose Marie done put in a new
   Valve cover gasket,
Them jeans good for a whole nother
   10,000 mile.

Man the wood them jeans cut,
And split and trucked and stacked,
   No wonder the axe
Been yearning and drooping
Like the poor lone gander
   For them old jeans.

Look out, get set, let
   The woods take warning,
   Come six in the morning
   Me and them jeans is back,
What I mean *ready*,
We going to *go*
And don't care nothing for nothing,
            baby,
   Not even the snow.

Simple

Looking back 25 years I
    imagine it simple
(the reality being so
    uselessly complex),

how we made a pier, a jetty
    of lights, a brightness
in that fantastic dark,
    down which we took our way

to the vessel that lay in the
    shadows. We stood
a moment, looking here or there,
    and then you stepped aboard

as if this were perfectly
    natural, and I turned
back into the knowledge of going
    crazy from loneliness.

The lights went out, the pier
    vanished, the vessel
became a kind of legend
    of a ship beating

Oriental seas. Looking
    back I imagine
how I retired to a room
    I built, perhaps

a kiva lit by reflections
  of the moon, where I
celebrated over and over
  the trembling mysteries

of loss. I became a living
  brain in an effigy
of reeds and cloth and paint,
  completely insane.

Late Sonnet

For that the sonnet no doubt was my own true
singing and suchlike other song, for that
I gave it up half-coldheartedly to set
my lines in a fashion that proclaimed its virtue
original in young arrogant artificers who
had not my geniality nor voice, and yet
their fashionableness was persuasive to me, — what
shame and sorrow I pay!
                                    And that I knew
that beautiful hot old man Sidney Bechet
and heard his music often but not what he
was saying, that tone, phrasing, and free play
of feeling mean more than originality,
these being the actual qualities of song.
Nor is it essential to be young.

Vermont

It's French, of course — our name. And I must think
(since nobody knows) the first to have uttered it
was Samuel de Champlain, an utter Frenchman;
the first as well to have seen our great green mountain;
or rather, first of the pallidly pigmented.
Yet truth to tell, not many of any color
were here before him. Meager is the word
for our prehistory; we are not rich
in relics, nor in much else, and that's a fact,
which may be why the divers kinds of diggers
prefer New Mexico and Arizona.
Well, the Algonquins lay to westward, Mic-macs
and their kin eastward, what else could Vermont,
hemmed in between two such antagonists,
ever expect to be but no man's land?
Or at best a land of passage. Warriors came,
hunters came (two who are one in nature),
came to make war and hunt and then go home,
those that survived. They didn't stay. They knew
our ponds and rivers, mountains and notches, knew
all our sublimities, yet somehow left
only their campfires smoldering into carbon
and a few skeletons moldering into garbage
for our three professional and thirteen amateur
archaeologists to ponder. But who'd ask more,
of either archaeologists or relics?
Not I. Vermont shares this much with my other
favorite country, Iceland, viz. that neither
required a dispossession for their conquest.
Iceland was there, pristine and uninhabited,
there for the taking; Vermont almost the same.
That's saying nothing, granted, for the auks,
those copperplate amiabilities who would have claimed
Iceland if they'd been asked, and nothing either

36

for the panthers, otters, moose, and wolverines,
and the pine trees of Vermont. What was it like,
this land of passage? Green. Remarkably green,
and not in summer only but all year round.
White pine was what the plant biologists call
our climax — nature's multimillennial orgasm —
especially on the mountains: trees as tall
as western pines, and brilliantly, brightly green.
No wonder Champlain, looking up at Mansfield
from his longboat over the windblown lake,
murmured "ver' mont" and wrote it on his map.
The best were blazed with the king's purple, to be
cut down, dragged by oxen to Otter Creek
or the Onion River or the Lamoille, and floated
into the lake and north to the St. Lawrence,
thence by ship to the royal navy yards.
Vermont white pine made the best mast in the world.
(India, Arnhem Land, have you seen our pines?)
The rest were burnt for potash. Now you'll hike
from Big Jay down to Pisgah and not see
a pine tree more than twelve rod tall. The valleys,
it's said, had plane trees (where they grow no more),
the foothills beech, then maple and butternut
on higher ground, birch by the ponds and brooks.
Et cetera. Speaking of water, maybe
the Yorkers have us beat, some say they do,
with Saranac's wild splendor. And yet, imagine
Willoughby back before the people came,
including Frost's Hill Wife (I wish I'd known her):
how the sun shone on that blue surface set
in its fringe of birch and fir, or how the mists
in early morning swirled between the cliffs
on either shore, with Wheeler Mountain dome
over beyond. I wish I'd seen it. I wish

I'd seen Vermont, the whole Vermont, just once
in that great classical time before the trees
departed, once so that I could see now
more clearly what it might have been. I know
what it is, a land of passage. Oh, there's some
who would deny it, seekers for what they call
their ''roots.'' But when our people began to come
they never stopped, and most were passing on.
The Allens and their breed, rough frontiersmen,
rum-drinkers and free-thinkers, you can't help
liking them, and yet you can't admire them,
speculators that they were, manipulators
of timber, potash, *land*. When Ethan stormed
Ticonderoga was he the patriot? Or
was he merely defending the several thousands
of square miles belonging to the Onion River
Land Company, which he and his brothers
had founded? Later, when it seemed he might
secure their holdings through a separate peace,
it's true, negotiations were begun,
secret negotiations, obscure meetings
with Britishers in Canada, and that's how
Vermont got started, this peculiar mixture —
heroism, hardship, greed. It never stopped.
The farmers came — that's what they called themselves —
who settled the Allens' speculative miles
and plowed the hillsides up and down for corn
until the hills wore out, and then brought sheep
to graze the weeds. And when the sheep wore out,
the farmers, worn out too, their women worn out,
died or contracted a religious contagion
or moved to Nevada and started over. Others
came too, the Irish, French-Canadians, those
who thought they were in luck to work a starved

and stony land, and maybe they were. The idle,
the rich, the developers, the ski-bums, the gamblers,
they all came, seasonal migrants. They blotted out
what was left of the green mountain to make
their ski-tows, hostels, and chalets. And now
they're set to build a dog track, so I'm told,
over in Georgia Plain — a dog track! That's
whippets and hounds chasing a tin rabbit. Maybe
Vermonters need that image of themselves.
For me, I swear I'd rather have cock-fighting
than dog-racing any time. At least the chickens
do what they do without a mechanical motive.

West Bolton is due north of Bolton, East
Burke is due south of Burke, and, yes, South Reading
is three-and-one-half miles northwest of Reading.
You might say Vermonters don't know where they're at.
"What's the difference, it's all Vermont." Granted.
And so wherever we are we claim our right
to name it: Calais rhymes with palace (only
there *is* no Calais, just East Calais and
West Calais, the center having vanished). Charlotte
is pronounced shallot; Berlin rhymes with Merlin;
Ely rhymes with Swahili. I admire
our independence, so do we all, seeing
there's not much else in this world to admire.
Vermont is what you might call a Society
for Independent Mutual Self-Admiration.
We've had two presidents. Chester A. Arthur
was born in Fairfield (some say Waterville,
but Fairfield's where they've built the "replica"
of the Arthur homestead, dreamed out of thin air,
the original having burnt up or sunk down
a good while before anyone noticed, so

Fairfield is where it is), and then passed on
to York state at an early age and never
set foot in Vermont again; Vermont's loss is
the nation's gain. Then there was Calvin Coolidge,
born in Plymouth and passed on there as well,
a remarkable steadfastness. Cal at heart
was a poet, perhaps our greatest native-born poet;
it's hard to tell though, Vermont not being
notably friendly to the arts. Her sons
are channeled into other callings. Cal
went into politics and took his poetry with him.
Who else has put the whole of modern history
into one line of suitable pentameter?
"The business of America is business."
Ethan would have approved that. As for me,
I wish I'd written it, though in my spirit.
I've mentioned Robert Frost already. He
was a Californian. Everyone knows he made
a good thing out of Vermont, and Vermont
is making a good thing out of him. His place
at Ripton is a tourist attraction only
somewhat less popular than skiing and well
ahead of the Joseph Smith Monument at
Royalton. Well, perhaps I wish I'd written
"The Hill Wife" too, though mainly I'm content
to read it once a year, and then a dozen
or fifteen other poems with it. No,
I'd not be Frost. The truth is, first, that finding
an honest-to-God Yankee son-of-a-bitch
is not easy, but when you've found one, look out! —
you've found a humdinger, maybe a Robert Frost;
second, that Frost has been a frightful burden
on all younger Vermont poets, who have spent years

fighting him off, until now at last we dare
approach nearer, a little, without the fear
of losing our own identities (poetry
is poetry, after all, and Vermont's Vermont);
and third, that recently the state's become
far more hospitable to poets — oh,
mind you, not native-born (Paul Blackburn from
St. Albans had to take his splendid talent
to New York City before he found a home),
yet many of us are here. Why, in this one district,
northwestern Vermont, there's Hewitt of New Jersey,
Broughton of Pennsylvania, Bass of Texas,
Edwards of Georgia, Engels of Michigan,
Budbill of Ohio, and Huddle of Virginia —
yes, and Kinnell of Rhode Island too, I'll stick
him in, ours by right though living a trifle
eastward, Sheffield way on the height-of-land —
and all twanging away in one or another fashion
of Yankee song, and all of us passing on.
Have I been too hard on Frost? Let's say I have.
Let's say he made, out of his own bad temper
and this forsaken and forsaking land,
a large part of our context. Not the whole,
not that by any means, but nevertheless
a large part. We must come to terms with him,
or find ourselves cut off completely. Frost,
whatever else you say, possessed a saving
curiosity. That's it, he got around,
he knew this people, he explored this land;
he saw, he apprehended, he perceived,
at least at his best he did, and by God that's
seven-eighths of the battle and five-eighths further
than most of us ever get. Once Ezra Pound
told me in a letter, or hollered rather,

"Curiosity, gorbloastit, kuryositty—
thass wot I'm tawkin abaout!" So bravo.
Bravissimo. Those two old enemies
had more between them, I expect, than either
would have been willing to allow. A hundred
years from now they'll almost look like friends.

I'm from Connecticut. But please, not Stamford,
not New Canaan. I'm a Litchfield man—
Litchfield County, that is—like Ethan Allen.
A speculator too? Some say I've farmed
this poetry hill for what it's worth. I could
offer extenuating circumstances,
my life has had them (and maybe not much more),
but truly now, what else could I have done,
being, or trying to be, a poet? That means a person
in the fullest sense. And does that mean in turn
something of a son-of-a-bitch? I think
Vermonters know, better than anything else,
just what a plus-and-minus tangle man is.
There was a man of Stowe who wondered which
mountain was higher, Mansfield or Camel's Hump,
until, maybe to win a bet, he climbed the peak
of Mansfield, loaded a ball without the wadding,
lay down and steadied his flintlock on a stone
and aimed at the ne plus ultra of Camel's Hump.
Sure enough, slowly the ball rolled forward
and dropped from the muzzle, a gratifying plop,
as I imagine, onto the alpine moss.
Mansfield was higher, and is, if by no more
than twenty rods. On the way down he killed
one bobcat for sport and two snowshoe hares
for the family pot. The only way I know
to do a thing is the directest way,

in art as elsewhere. (Though that's not to say
the imagination in a particular work
may not choose indirection.) Vermonters take
the directest way in everything but speech.
I knew a woman once in Beebe Plain
that had an idiot girl she kept at home
and dressed and fed and babied till the girl
was thirty-five in years and nigh in heft
to two sacks of hog ration. Bess, what for,
they asked her more than once, how come you don't
put her out with the state or in a home?
Bess'd look straight and answer, "Hell, I know
her feed's worth more than she is, which is nothing,
and that don't take in the labor — mine, that is.
I guess I'm used to her, is all. Besides,
if she wan't here who would there be to show me
how smart I am?" That's how she spoke her feelings.
It's something like our feelings for Vermont.

Those Indians who came and didn't stay,
no doubt they had their business, yet they were
in one sense tourists. Did they lay a curse
on our green mountain (like many a tourist since
who's et our beans)? Nobody would blame them,
and something must account for our obsession
with snatching dollars out of strangers' pockets.
Down in Montpelier the state development
commission spends a hundred grand a year —
which is not hay, by God — in advertising
our sleepy farmlands and our quaint red barns,
but not one cent to keep our farmers eating
or those barns standing. How can New England farms
compete with those monster western corporations?
We need a new crop, something that will grow

on hillsides, and on granite hillsides at that.
There was a fellow over in Underhill
who ranched musk oxen and proved it could be done,
but do you think the state would lend a hand?
My own idea that I've been working on
is a neat machine that will exactly crack
butternuts so the meat will come out whole.
Oh, there's a market for them. Rose Marie
knows eighteen recipes. But cracking them —
the butternuts, that is, though Rose Marie's
handwriting can be pretty near as hard —
takes hammer and anvil, and generally it means
bloody fingers and nutshells in your cookies
and a visit to the dentist. Who needs that?
Well, all I need is *half* a hundred grand.
That's all; no more. Think what the state would save.
And I'd have just enough to get me started
and work out a few bugs in my neat machine.
Then what? Easy. I'd make all Butternut Mountain
one huge farm and then hire half the town
at harvest time, which would just nicely fill
that slack, fidgetty season after the cider
has been put down to work and everyone
is sitting around uptight, waiting to test it.

Republicans? We've got a few. In fact
that's damned near *all* we had for a hundred years.
Then in '64 we went for the Democrats,
the first time, went for the lesser evil
(that's what we thought) and gave our vote to Johnson
against Goldwater, and you can bet we won't
make that mistake again. Right now we have
a Democrat for governor, which isn't
a mistake exactly, it's an aberration.

44

I don't know if it's true, but I've been told
the poor guy suffers so from loneliness
down there in Montpelier he has to call
a press conference just so he can find
someone to talk to. Mind, I don't say it's true.
Vermonters are Republicans because
Bostonians are Democrats, that's all.
That's enough. Still there are Republicans
and Republicans. Take New Hampshire,
for instance; over there if you object
to the divine right of state senators
you're a Communist. Why hell, I knew a man
living in Coos Junction who wouldn't take
a twenty dollar bill; he couldn't stand
to carry Andrew Jackson in his pocket.
"Gimme two tens," he said. "Ain't it just like
them fathead red-tape artists? They design
the twenty for a red, then put a great man
like Hamilton on the tens." As far as I know
there's only one hereditary senator
in Vermont, and that's Fred Westphal from over
Elmore Mountain way. I don't know for sure
how Fred feels about Andy Jackson, but
he's carrying Elmore in his pocket and the rest
of his district too. Fred told a friend of mine
he'd never kissed a baby's face or a voter's
ass. I expect that's right. Of course it's not
exactly saying what he has done either
to keep himself down there in the legislature
since God knows when. "He's drawed his pay and 'tother
perquisites" — that's what my neighbor says.
My neighbor's an anarchist. That is to say,
a Vermonter, and that's to say, a Republican.

But just because he goes by the same label
as Nelson Rockefeller doesn't mean the two
have anything in common. They're worlds apart —
worlds. Ask my neighbor how he feels about
the government — the State with a capital S —
and what comes back is pure Bakuninism,
only of course with due allowances for different
times, places, idioms, and temperaments.
''Sons-of-bitches, every one of them'' — that's
his feeling, and he means Rockefeller too,
or maybe especially. Why, I suspect
even Fred Westphal might be an anarchist,
though he'd turn the color of Ed Wipprecht's
best red cabbage if you accused him of it.
For my part, what's the use of stalling? I'm
an anarchist, have been for forty years,
only more a Warrenite than Bakuninite,
which is to say, nonviolent and independent,
or in other words American, which is what
lets me remain a patriot and a son
of the Founding Fathers, like my friend Paul Goodman —
Paul, the city Jew-boy who worked and fought
in New York all his life, fighting for virtue
or even for reason in an evil, crazy city,
and lost, and was always losing, which was why
he liked the country maybe and called his poems
hawkweeds and died three summers past — no, four —
over in Stratford underneath Percy Mountain.
The point is, there's a losing kind of man
who still will save this world if anybody
can save it, who believes. . .oh, many things,
that horses, say, are fundamentally preferable
to tractors, that small is more likable than big,
and that human beings work better and last longer

when they're free. Call him an anarchist,
call him what you will, a humanist,
an existentialist, hell, a Republican — names
are slippery, unreliable things. And yet
call him a Vermonter. That's what he is.

I don't say you can't find him in New Hampshire,
or even Maine — or Australia, for all I know —
the loser, the forlorn believer, the passer on.
But old Vermont is where I've found him mainly,
on the green mountain — on the western slope of it
if you want to be particular — where we talk
with that strange dialect which isn't exactly
Yankee, nor exactly anything else either.
"Calful" we say (as in *calf*), not "cahful,"
certainly not "careful," and what we make
our livings on, milking them morning and night,
are "kyeous." O.k. The further point is this:
we are still here, although we're passing on.
You won't hear much about us, but we're here.
I think we are the last true regionalists,
or maybe — who knows? — the first of a new breed.
Not local colorists, at any rate, not keepers
of quaintness for quaintness's sake. We're realists.
And realism means place, and place means
where we are. We name it, with all its garbage
and slaughter, and its comeliness too, and then
it is our center — where we are. We try,
in our own unobtrusive way, to make it
a center of everywhere, a center *for*
everywhere (and thanks to Ted Enslin of Maine
for saying that). I think and I do believe
we know the way to glory, or to what can be
glory for this worn-down bedraggled race —

peace, freedom, losing, and passing on. And place.
We know it if anyone would listen. Most likely
anyone won't. Anyone never has.

Well, I've said that Robert Frost had curiosity
and took the trouble to go and satisfy it,
on foot or driving that bay mare of his;
he saw the state, he met the people. Yet
my guess is that he traveled by himself.
Your typical Vermonter is a man
of, say, sufficient winters, or a woman
for that matter, walking the back roads,
the pastures, woodlots, hills, and brooks, alone
or with a dog, mostly looking down.
Curiosity? Yes, but it bears inward
as much as outward, maybe more. My dog
is Locky, a mixed-breed bitch, though shepherd
predominates, and in her eleven years
Locky and I have walked these thousand acres
ten thousand times, I reckon. Do you think
we go on sniffing the same old rabbit trail,
examining the same old yellow birch
forever? We grow stiff. We plod now, I
with my stick, Locky with her lame forepaw,
and mostly we look down. And so did Frost.
Which brings me to the "all-important question."
What is the difference, now at last, between
the contemporary and the archaic? I
say "drawed" for "drew" and "deef" for "deaf" and still
use "shall" and "shan't" in ordinary conversation
like any good Vermonter, and sometimes too
I write "thou" for "you." So am I therefore
dead? That will come soon enough. Meanwhile
my language is mine, I insist on it,

a living language as long as it is spoken
by living men and women naturally,
as long as it is used. And so with manners,
styles, attitudes, the whole spectrum of appearance.
As for the unappearing, the soul, what further
need or can be said? It is my own.
No, I believe this difference was concocted
in New York City, that necropolis,
city of critics and city of fashion, which is
saying the same thing. It is a place to stay.
But genuine regionalism is not fixation,
not in either sense; it is awareness
of passing on. I don't speak paradox,
I speak for once directly. Place is the now
which is eternal. And we are passing on.
The name of our green mountain is from French,
but sometimes, ungallicly, we twist it, saying
Vérmont with the stress up front. We intend
no harm and only characteristic disrespect.
Once when I heard it I was struck by how
the name might be divided differently,
Verm-ont, the Worm of Being. We are torn
here in this place that is our now between
its beauty and its depravity. The beauty
is mostly old, our mountains and our farms,
and the depravity is mostly new.
We don't hate it exactly, being not
the hate-conceiving kind, but we despair.
God, we despair! — Vermont's protracted gloom,
our end-of-the-winter desolation, April
in our cold hearts. From this we make ourselves,
remake ourselves each moment, stronger, harder,
with our own beauty. Yes, our great green mountain
is the worm of being, long and irregular,

twined lengthwise through our state, our place, our now.
Meanwhile we dream of other, sunnier places.
Myself, I'm going down next month to look
at a house I know of in New Mexico.

John Dryden

Dry they call him, and dry is what he hopes
never to be, though springwater is all his drink
six nights after the welfare comes, and most
all his feed too, I sometimes think — though once
I saw him bring down a hare at seven rods
with a stone, and it didn't look lucky either.
When I asked him if he knew a famous poet
had the same name, he looked at me not quite
contemptuously; and yet I took a while to see
his scorn wasn't because he was smarter than I'd
credited — for a fact he can't read but about
half what's printed on the welfare check — but rather
because he'd been asked so damn many times before,
and he figured I should have known. I should have too.
Dry is not dumb. He's only crazy. Well, anyway
that's the general impression around the Plot,
which is what they call this section. My neighbor
rounds up her kids and locks her door when Dry
comes striding and caroling up the hill from town
in his outsize rummage pants with a carton
of grub held like an offering in both arms and his coat
gone slanty-wise from the fifth of sauterne
in his pocket. Paranoid, I'd say. There's more
than a few in these mountains, and sometimes I'm not
just certain about myself. But I know Dry.
I know he hasn't worked four consecutive days
on any one job in fifteen years. That's
indicative. Once we were haying up at Marshall's
and Dry took offense, we never knew what for,
and came after Marshall and me with his hayfork,
chasing us round the tractor, his face dead white
like snow that's thawed and frozen again; he did,

and it wasn't funny either. My kidneys ached
two hours after from thinking about that fork.
Finally he saw he couldn't catch us. He threw down
the fork and marched off, straight as a bee, over
the meadow, the pasture, the orchard, the fence, and
                    was gone.
That year Marshall and I made the rest of the hay
alone. One time Gilbert told how he and Dry
were cutting sugarwood for old man Saunders
up toward Codding Hollow, and Dry took one
of his spells and came after Gilbert with the axe,
and Gilbert yanked quick on his chainsaw string and
                    remarked,
"Dry, you damn fool, listen here — just you set down
that thing, or by the jumping Jesus Christ
I'll cut off both your arms." Dry set it down,
about three inches into a black birch stump, and marched
straight as a bee over brakes and brambles,
hobblebush and thornapple, and he was gone.
Which may be indicative too; he can be "took"
right sudden, but when he's licked he knows it.
And he's a fair hand at marching. He told me once
how it was here forty years back. "Them days
was cruel," he said, "awful cruel. Things was
turning on a slow reel" — and he made a motion
like so, like the bobbins down in the woollen mill
when they run half-speed. "Why, hell," he said,
"I had one of them five dollar gold certificates,
you remember? I felt like I was rich, and I was too,
but I spent it running some cunt. And it come back,
and I spent it again, and it come back again,
so help me over and over till the damn thing
wore itself out — I carried the pieces for years.
But they're gone now." One time Dry vanished,

clean gone, no one knew where and don't know yet,
but when he came back I met him up in the woods
and he stood on a spruce log and threw out his arms
and said, ''God, Hayden, it's Moxie in the can,
being back on this here goddamn mountain again!''
And he laughed. The last what you could call steady
job Dry had, as far as I know, was 1945
down at the rendering plant in Burlington where he
slugged cows with an axe and pushed their guts
through a hole in the floor all day. ''Stink? Jesus,
I guess I stunk! Like a she bear in whistling time,
but I made good money. Forty a week, and that
wan't bad in them days; but I spent it all
running the cunt, every dime. Why, I got
throwed out of five flea-bag rooming houses just
from owing the rent.'' Running's what we say
a bull does when you turn him out to pasture
with the cows, so you can see how Dry felt about that —
leastways providing you've ever seen a bull
in action. ''But now, goddamn it'' — Dry spit
and grinned sly-like with his uppers, which is all
the teeth I've ever seen him wear — ''now
you could lay a slobbering big juicy one right there,
right there ready and open'' — him leaning and making
a kind of slicing gesture along the log —
''and I couldn't do nothing, I couldn't touch it,
couldn't hardly spit on it,'' and he spit and grinned.
''It'd be all wasted, Hayden. I'm fucked, fucked,
and I ain't but fifty-nine — how old are you?''
That's Dry, that's him, the nailhead every time.

Well, he lives up in the old Connell sugarhouse now
that he's shingled all over with sap bucket covers
to keep the wind out, till it looks like a big tin fish

in the pines by the crooked brook, and there's plenty
more he could tell you, like how he got bit that time
by the cattle grub and took the "purple aguey,"
or how he has a buckshot in him that keeps going
round and round in his veins, catching him sharp-like
on his cotterbone when he don't expect it
every now and again, or how he eats forty aspirins
a day and hears sweet potato music in his ears,
or how he fell in a cellarhole at blackberry time
and landed on a bear — "I says, 'Whuff, old bear,
get you away from me,' and then I climm the hell
out of there" — or how . . . but have you noticed
I can't talk *about* him without talking *like* him?
That's my trouble. Somehow I always seem
to turn into the other guy, and Dry's the kind
that brings it out the strongest. But *his* trouble
is what I'm telling about now; for it's not
just buckshot in his blood, it's worse, a whole
lot worse. His reel is turning slower and slower,
no mistake. Crazy? I reckon he is. I sure don't
want to be there when he's took bad, even now —
if he's got a fork or an axe within grabbing distance.
But I'll go up to call on him in his sugarhouse.
I believe old Dry is preparing to march again,
or anyway preparing to prepare. And I believe
he'll go straight as a bee, white as a squall of snow,
knowing what he damn well knows, over
the goldenrod, the birchwoods, the pines and hemlocks,
over the mountain. And he'll be gone. And then
Marshall and I shall make this hay alone,
by God, and curse old Dry. But in our thoughts
we'll remember and remember how that man could
        march.

Johnny Spain's White Heifer

The first time I saw Johnny Spain was
the first day I ever came to this town. There
he was, lantern jaw and broken nose, wall-eyed and
fractious, with a can of beer in one hand and a
walkie-talkie in the other, out in front
of the post office. And I heard someone saying,
"Johnny, what in hell are you doing?" "I'm looking,"
he answered, in an executive tone, "for me goddamn
white heifer." "Run off, did she?" "Yass,"
he said. "Busted me south-side fence, the bitch —
if some thieving bastard didn't bust it for her."
"You reckon she's running loose on Main Street?"
Johnny looked down, then up, then sideways, or possibly
all three together. "Hell, no," he growled.
"She's off there somewheres." He swung his beer can
in a circle. "Me boys is up in the hills, looking.
I'm di-recting the search." Then he turned away
to a crackle on the walkie-talkie.
                                    And that
was how Johnny liked it. He wasn't much
on farming, although his farm could have been
a fine one — closest to town, up on the hillside
overlooking the feed mill. But Johnny's curse
was a taste for administration. The "farm" was no more
than a falling-down barn, some mixed head
of cattle, and a flock of muddy ducks. Johnny
was the first man in the volunteer fire department
to have one of those revolving blue lights
set up on top of his car, and Johnny Spain
was *always* going to a fire. When he came down
off that hill of his in that air-borne '65 Pontiac —
look out! It was every man for himself

when Johnny was on the highway.
                              I used to think
sometimes I had a glimpse of that white heifer
that Johnny never found. "A goddamn beauty,"
he'd say. "By Jesus, she was. Why, I give
five whole greenback dollars cash and a pair
of Indian runners to Blueball Baxter for her
when she were a calf — there wan't a finer heifer
in the whole goddamn country." I'd see a flash
of white in the balsams at the upper end of the pasture
or in the thickets across the brook when I looked up
at twilight; but I never found her. Probably
all I saw was a deer-tail flashing.
                              After
they changed the town dump into a sanitary
land fill operation the selectmen hired Johnny
for custodian, and they gave him a little Michigan
dozer to bury the trash with. Johnny loved it.
"Dump it over there," he'd holler. "Goddamn it,
can't you see the sign? Tires and metal
go on the other side." One time he even
inaugurated a system of identification cards,
so people from Centerville and Irishtown
would quit using our dump, and by God
you had to show your pass, even if Johnny
had known you for years. Part of the deal
was salvage, of course. Johnny could take
whatever he wanted from the accumulated junk
and sell it. Trouble was he mostly didn't
or couldn't sell it, so it wound up in his
barnyard, everything from busted baby carriages
to stacks of old lard kegs from the diner,
up there to be viewed by whoever cared to look.
And the one with the best view was Mel Barstow,

son of the mill owner, who lived on the hill
above the other side of town. There they were,
two barons above the burg, facing each other
at opposite ends, like the West Wind and the East Wind
on an old-time map. Mel had everything
he thought he wanted — a home like a two-page spread
in *House and Garden*, for instance, and a wife
that was anyone's envy, and a pair of binoculars
with which he liked to watch the gulls flying
over the river. Of course he'd seen Johnny's place
many a time, but one evening he focused down
on that barnyard, then quick got on the phone.
"Johnny, why in hell don't you clean up that mess
over there? It's awful. It's a disgrace." Johnny
didn't say much. But a couple of nights later,
maybe an hour past dark, he phoned up Mel.
"Mel," he said, "I got me a pair of them by-
nockyewlars over to Morrisville this forenoon,
and I been a-studying them goddamn birds out there,
and what I want to know is why in the hell
you don't tell that good-looking female of yours
to put some clothes on her backside when she's parading
up and down behind that picture window? Picture, hell —
I'll say it's a picture! It's a goddamn frigging
dis-grace, if you want to know the truth."
                                        Well,
I expect for a while Mel's wife was the one
that would have liked to get lost, and maybe
Mel too, because it's a cinch you can't go down
to buy even a pack of Winstons at the IGA
without running into Johnny Spain, and of course
Johnny's the one that knows exactly, exactly
how to keep the sting alive, winking wall-eyed
both ways at once, grinning that three-toothed grin.

But Johnny Spain's white heifer was what was lost.
She wasn't found. Wherever she is, she's gone.
Oh, I'm not the only one who thought they saw her,
because reports kept coming in, all the way round
from the Old Settlement clear up to Mariveau's
gravel pit. But that's all they were, just
reports. She'd have made a first-rate cow,
I reckon, if a man could have caught her, only
of course somewhat more than a mite wild.

Lady

Lady they calls me, Lady and they always has
my whole life long, and I hated it — God, how I
hated it! You know? But you can't go hating
on a thing like that forever. One time I says,
"What the hell's the difference?" Now they call me
Lady, same as ever, and that's o.k.,
now my belly don't even twitch like it used to.
Hating. That for those other downcountry folk,
that's for your city folk. What does it get them?
Gut-ache. Anybody knows that.
                    Well, what I've got
is this nice old house now, big barn and the shed,
a first-rate meadow, some fair hill pasture,
and a woodlot that's good enough for what I need.
And my horses, my Arabians, every one bred
by my own stallion; yes, and them there silver
whoduddies you see on the mantel for showing
all over the state. I got me my Herefords too,
registered, fourteen head. And I got me a job,
to make up what the horses and beef won't bring,
down to the hospital in Waterbury. You know?
The *mental* hospital. Don't get the idea I'm one
of those movie battleaxe types neither. I'm not.
I work at the ward for the chronics on the midnight shift,
and there's a good lot of them poor bastards in there
as can't sleep when it comes night, and I know why.
Believe me, I know why. I treat them right.
I talk to them, make them tell me their stories,
and then sometimes they can sleep. Sometimes.
Then I come home and do my chores and sleep
myself. Later I make hay, or mend fence, or tend
the foals, or whatever needs doing. I got me
a Ford 3000 tractor, a baler, mower, side-rake, a Dodge

two-ton platform truck, and when I need something else,
like a tedder or a teakle rig, I borrows it.
We're neighborly round here, we have to be. Why,
we switch off labor for all our big jobs. Yes, sir.
And I do my share.
                              One time I was spreading
manure down in the lower pasture, next the spruces.
I was late, see, past sundown, because I can tell you
I got to run seventy minutes to the hour to work
this place. And of course that had to be the time
the damn spreader jams, so there's nothing to do
but throw out the stuff by hand. I was just climbing
off of the tractor with the dung fork in one hand
when this old she bear come out of the trees. Popped
right out of there, coming right at me, big
as a spruce-oil kiln, she looked, and black as a stove.
I whooped, let me tell you, and threw my fork
and climm back on that tractor in a kind of a hurry,
breathing a mite hard. And when I got back to the barn
I found I had more manure than I started out with.

I told Jasper the next day. He owns that
gone-to-Boston-looking place over the hill
with the bam-o-gilly in the dooryard. ''Jas,''
I says, ''I was plain *scart* — scart of that old she bear.
I shit my britches.'' Jas, he looked straight and soft-like.
''Lady,'' he says, ''I don't blame you none. 'Twas me
I believe I'd of shatten too.''
                              That's one thing —
small, it don't mean much. You asked me who I was.
I'm Lady. I'm what some folk might call
uncommon, a speck maybe. Well, I get along,
a good neighbor to good neighbors. There's all kinds
living round these mountains. I raise beef,

a little, and I raise some damn fine horses, here
on this hilltop farm, then I work out nights
in the loony-bin. That's all, mostly. Though sometimes
it does seem funny, don't it, the way things happen.

Marshall Washer

They are cowshit farmers, these New Englanders
who built our red barns so admired as emblems,
in photograph, in paint, of America's imagined
past (backward utopians that we've become).
But let me tell how it is inside those barns.
Warm. Even in dead of winter, even in the
dark night solid with thirty below, thanks
to huge bodies breathing heat and grain sacks
stuffed under doors and in broken windows, warm,
and heaped with reeking, steaming manure, running
with urine that reeks even more, the wooden channels
and flagged aisles saturated with a century's
excreta. In dim light, with scraper and shovel,
the manure is lifted into a barrow or a trolley
(suspended from a ceiling track), and moved
to the spreader—half a ton at a time. Grain
and hay are distributed in the mangers, bedding
of sawdust strewn on the floor. The young cattle
and horses, separately stabled, are tended. The cows
are milked; the milk is strained and poured
in the bulk tank; the machines and all utensils
are washed with disinfectant. This, which is called
the "evening chores," takes about three hours.
Next morning, do it again. Then after breakfast
hitch the manure spreader to the old Ferguson
and draw it to the meadows, where the manure
is kicked by mechanical beaters onto the snow.
When the snow becomes too deep for the tractor,
often about mid-January, then load the manure
on a horse-drawn sled and pitch it out by hand.
When the snow becomes too deep for the horses

make your dung heap behind the barn. Yes, a good
winter means no dung heap; but a bad one
may mean a heap as big as a house. And so,
so, night and morning and day, 365 days
a year until you are dead: this is part
of what you must do. Notice how many times
I have said "manure"? It is serious business.
It breaks the farmers' backs. It makes their land.
It is the link eternal, binding man and beast
and earth. Yet our farmers still sometimes say
of themselves, derogatively, that they are "cowshit
farmers."

2

      I see a man with a low-bent back
driving a tractor in stinging rain, or just as he
enters a doorway in his sheepskin and enormous
mittens, stomping snow from his boots, raising
his fogged glasses. I see a man in bib overalls
and rubber boots kneeling in cowshit to smear
ointment on a sore teat, a man with a hayfork,
a dungfork, an axe, a 20-pound maul
for driving posts, a canthook, a grease gun.
I see a man notching a cedar post
with a double-bladed axe, rolling the post
under his foot in the grass: quick strokes and there
is a ringed groove one inch across, as clean
as if cut with the router blade down at the mill.
I see a man who drags a dead calf or watches
a barn roaring with fire and thirteen heifers
inside, I see his helpless eyes. He has stood
helpless often, of course: when his wife died
from congenital heart disease a few months before
open-heart surgery came to Vermont, when his sons

departed, caring little for the farm because
he had educated them — he who left school
in 1931 to work by his father's side
on an impoverished farm in an impoverished time.
I see a man who studied by lamplight, the journals
and bulletins, new methods, struggling to buy
equipment, forty years to make his farm
a good one; alone now, his farm the last
on Clay Hill, where I myself remember ten.
He says "I didn't mind it" for "I didn't notice it,"
"dreened" for "drained," "climb" (pronounced *climm*)
for "climbed," "stanchel" for "stanchion,"
and many other unfamiliar locutions; but I
have looked them up, they are in the dictionary,
standard speech of lost times. He is rooted
in history as in the land, the only man I know
who lives in the house where he was born. I see
a man alone walking his fields and woods,
knowing every useful thing about them, moving
in a texture of memory that sustains his lifetime
and his father's lifetime. I see a man
falling asleep at night with thoughts and dreams
I could not infer — and would not if I could —
in his chair in front of his television.

3

                        I have written
of Marshall often, for his presence is in my poems
as in my life, so familiar that it is not named;
yet I have named him sometimes too, in writing
as in life, gratefully. We are friends. Our friendship
began when I came here years ago, seeking
what I had once known in southern New England,
now destroyed. I found it in Marshall, among others.

64

He is friend and neighbor both, an important
distinction. His farm is one-hundred-eighty acres
(plus a separate woodlot of forty more), and one
of the best-looking farms I know, sloping smooth
pastures, elm-shaded knolls, a brook, a pond,
his woods of spruce and pine, with maples and oaks
along the road — not a showplace, not by any means,
but a working farm with fences of old barbed wire;
no pickets, no post-and-rail. His cows are Jerseys.
My place, no farm at all, is a country laborer's
holding, fourteen acres ''more or less'' (as the deed
says), but we adjoin. We have no fence. Marshall's
cows graze in my pasture; I cut my fuel
in his woods. That's neighborliness. And when
I came here Marshall taught me. . . I don't know,
it seems like everything: how to run a barn,
make hay, build a wall, make maple syrup
without a trace of bitterness, a thousand things.
(Though I thought I wasn't ignorant when I came,
and I wasn't — just three-quarters informed.
You know how good a calf is, born three-legged.)
In fact half my life now, I mean literally half,
is spent in actions I could not perform without
his teaching. Yet it wasn't teaching; he *showed* me.
Which is what makes all the difference. In return
I gave a hand, helped in the fields, started
frozen engines, mended fence, searched for lost calves,
picked apples for the cider mill, and so on.
And Marshall, alone now, often shared my table.
This too is neighborliness.

4

As for friendship,
what can I say where words historically fail?

It is something else, something more difficult. Not
western affability, at any rate, that tells
in ten minutes the accommodation of its wife's — well,
you know. Yankees are independent, meaning
individual and strong-minded but also private;
in fact private first of all. Marshall and I
worked ten years together, and more than once
in hardship. I remember the late January
when his main gave out and we carried water,
hundreds and thousands of gallons, to the heifers
in the upper barn (the one that burned next summer),
then worked inside the well to clear the line
in temperatures that rose to ten below
at noonday. We knew such times. Yet never
did Marshall say the thought that was closest to him.
Privacy is what this is; not reticence, not
minding one's own business, but a positive sense
of the secret inner man, the sacred identity.
A man is his totem, the animal of his mind.
Yet I was angered sometimes. How could friendship
share a base so small of mutual substance?
Unconsciously I had taken friendship's measure
from artists elsewhere who had been close to me,
people living for the minutest public dissection
of emotion and belief. But more warmth was,
and is, in Marshall's quiet ''hello'' than in all
those others and their wordiest protestations,
more warmth and far less vanity.

5

                              He sows
his millet broadcast, swinging left to right,
a half-acre for the cows' ''fall tonic'' before
they go in the barn for good; an easy motion,

slow swinging, a slow dance in the field, and just
the opposite, right to left, for the scythe
or the brush-hook. Yes, I have seen such dancing
by a man alone in the slant of the afternoon.
At his anvil with his big smith's hammer
he can pound shape back in a wagon iron, or tap
a butternut so it just lies open. When he skids
a pine log out of the woods he stands in front
of his horse and hollers, ''Gee-up, goddamn it,''
''Back, you ornery son-of-a-bitch,'' and then
when the chain rattles loose and the log settles
on the stage, he slicks down the horse's sweaty
neck and pulls his ears. In October he eases
the potatoes out of the ground in their rows,
gentle with the potato-hook, then leans and takes
a big one in his hand, and rubs it clean
with his thumbs, and smells it, and looks
along the new-turned frosty earth to fields,
to hills, to the mountain, forests in their color
each fall no less awesome. And when in June
the mowing time comes around and he fits the wicked
cutter-bar to the Ferguson, he shuts the cats
indoors, the dogs in the barn, and warns
the neighbors too, because once years ago,
many years, he cut off a cat's legs in the tall
timothy. To this day you can see him
squirm inside when he tells it, as he must tell it,
obsessively, June after June. He is tall,
a little gray, a little stooped, his eyes
crinkled with smile-lines, both dog-teeth gone.
He has worn his gold-rimmed spectacles so long
he looks disfigured when they're broken.

6

No doubt
Marshall's sorrow is the same as human
sorrow generally, but there is this
difference. To live in a doomed city, a doomed
nation, a doomed world is desolating, and we all,
all are desolated. But to live on a doomed farm
is worse. It must be worse. There the exact
point of connection, gate of conversion, is —
mind and life. The hilltop farms are going.
Bottomland farms, mechanized, are all that survive.
As more and more developers take over
northern Vermont, values of land increase,
taxes increase, farming is an obsolete vocation —
while half the world goes hungry. Marshall walks
his fields and woods, knowing every useful thing
about them, and knowing his knowledge useless.
Bulldozers, at least of the imagination,
are poised to level every knoll, to strip bare
every pasture. Or maybe a rich man will buy it
for a summer place. Either way the link
of the manure, that had seemed eternal, is broken.
Marshall is not young now. And though I am only
six or seven years his junior, I wish somehow
I could buy the place, merely to assure him
that for these few added years it might continue —
drought, flood, or depression. But I am too
ignorant, in spite of his teaching. This is more
than a technocratic question. I cannot smile
his quick sly Yankee smile in sorrow,
nor harden my eyes with the true granitic resistance
that shaped this land. How can I learn the things
that are not transmissible? Marshall knows them.
He possesses them, the remnant of human worth
to admire in this world, and I think to envy.

Crows Mark

They don't say gully, cove, cut, gulch,
glen, dell, etc., around here,
they call it a gulf, meaning
something less than a notch but more
than a ravine, and my house sits
in the bottom of Foote Brook Gulf. Back
about a hundred twenty years or so
the house was a barn, more like a shed,
a utility building
attached to a sawmill on the brook.
Well, all the mill that's left now
is part of the old foundation, but the shed
was converted into a house by tacking on a smaller
shed — I can show you where they toed in
the spikes through the two wall plates —
to serve as a kitchen. It still does.
The house is called Crows Mark. Don't ask me
why. I know, but I'm tired of telling.

It's a south-running brook, the Foote, rising
back up on the beaver meadows
on Butternut Mountain, which means
the Gulf runs north-south too,
roughly; and this in turn means the winter wind
that's usually more west than north sails
overhead — we hear it, a roar in the trees above,
but we don't feel it. Why, I've seen sheets
of snow flung over us, flopping and flapping,
and we dead calm underneath. Of course Marshall,
in his farmhouse up on the crest, gets it
full blast, so it's a good day's work to walk

from the house to the barn sometimes,
it seems as though. On the other hand,
still nights in winter the cold
spills down, over the pastures, the ledges,
into the Gulf till it's thirty-five
below on my thermometer, while Marshall
sits snug and comfy in the warmth
of the upper air where it's only twenty-five
under the zero, as I make sure
to point out to him next morning.
                                    And then sometimes,
usually ten or twelve nights a winter,
the wind veers round due north, straight
down from the pole, and when it hits the Gulf
it's like full choke on a twelve-gauge
barrel—compression, you know what I mean?
I mind one time
in January—'sixty-eight, I think it was—
the wind blew the beam of my flashlight
twice around the maple by the woodshed
and wrapped it tight. You don't
believe me? Ask Marshall. The flashlight
was hanging there still next morning.
I let it stay till the batteries wore out
and it fell down.
                            Fortunately the wind
at Crows Mark sits mostly west by north,
through the Waterville notch, over our heads.

The Poet

All night his window
shines in the woods
shadowed under the hills
where the gray owl

is hunting. He hears
the woodmouse scream —
so small a sound
in the great darkness

entering his pain.
For he is all and all
of pain, attracting
every new injury

to be taken and borne
as he must take
and bear it. He is
nothing; he is

his admiration. So
they seem almost
to know — the woodmouse
and the roving owl,

the woods and hills.
All night they move
around the stillness
of the poet's light.

Essay on Love

Years. Many years. Friends laugh, including
even my best friend, Rose Marie, but they all
    are younger, and I might laugh as well
      to think how they will

come to know. Or tears might be as easy.
I used to drive this wedge in the maple blocks
    with pleasure; now I wouldn't care
      if I never saw another.

Yet the air so clear, utterly clear, and the blue
September sky arching the forest's bright crown
    so very deep: come, lean the sledge
      on its maple block

and walk away, slow, stepping by the little brook
where shad leaves turn coral and the turtlehead
    blooms, late this year, its petals
      still perfect and white.

See, ladies' tresses, right here where they always
were; kneel then to their fragrance, near
    to the cool of earth. And goldenrod,
      plumes of yellow

where yellow bees mumble, and asters, blue
and purple and white, New England asters
    that are our stars, and the small
      speckled asters, massed

at the edge of the clearing, that are called
farewell-to-summer; and there beneath them
　　the peeping, deep, blue, shy eyes
　　　　of the gentian,

so rare a color. Does that mean something? Count
the maple leaves if you can. Or those bluebirds
　　perched, one by one, apart, on the wire
　　　　over there, seven

blue in the sunlight: are they a rarity? Then
count too, as one always must, the ''rare'' pains,
　　hernia raving, bladder and penis
　　　　in an acid flame,

arthritic hip — was it Plato said a man
is finished at fifty-five? And Rose Marie,
　　my dear friend, whose spine is a pain
　　　　that I see marching

often enough in her young eyes. What do
the bluebirds say? They don't know why they wear
　　that rare color, or why they gather now
　　　　on that wire to fly

tomorrow to Guatemala; they don't know,
nor do I. Those seven little blue machines
　　look down from their pain on a somewhat
　　　　larger machine

of a somewhat less determinate color, down
into the clearing among coral shadblow leaves
　　and the red and golden maple leaves
　　　　and the parchment leaves

of moosewood, the speckled banks of asters.
Year, years; seasons and changes. Time,
   which is nothing but the measure of change —
      nothing, no meaning.

Years, years I've driven this wedge with my big
hammer into these maple blocks for Rose Marie,
   to keep her warm and give her stovewood
      for her kitchen

all winter, firesticks wrenched, split, pried
apart, each with the thought of her. I see
   so clearly, precisely, with the keen
      eyes of dispassion,

the trees, flowers, birds, all colors and forms,
but what good is such seeing in this chaos
   we used to call our order? She
      is invisible now,

a purity, the greater loveliness for the greater
seeing. Back to the block then, back once more,
   pick up the sledge, eyes down, and bend,
      bend to the labor

that is the only meaning. Farewell to summer.
Yes, let changes keep the time. I'll count
   no further, except these firesticks
      counted for her.

Alba

(*Good Friday, 1974*)

At this hour the refrigerator throbs,
             it does not hum.
Is this the refrigerator?
             Alba lux is throbbing, dilating
tremulous from behind the mountain,
             the premonitory glow, colorless,
and the mirror is dark.
             Whose face is there, whose —
pallid and blear?
             This throbbing is the house
of the day's meat, colorless flesh,
             to be eaten again, always.
Missa solemnis over the world
             spreading, light unto dark,
light on the dirty snow of April,
             on the face in the snow-mirror,
'till the watchman on the tower cry,
             oh, oh, there were times and times,
music in the light, leaves in the play of light.
             Wouldst thou hear what words can say
in a little? Reader,
             whose words are these? What
pronoun must be inserted here
             in bower, in flower?
Io, Isis! Hathor! *that sometime did. . .*
             with naked foot. . .
And so much joy was expended,
             yes, even the decade of anguish,
music and the thought that was music,
             golden lads and girls all must. . .

Watchman, who will be hanged today?
          The mirror melts, the snow seeps,
and the meat in the house, colorless, stirs
          and rises into lifelikeness,
a world throbs, the monotone
          solemn and meaningless —
without meaning,
          the eating, the eaten.
Was there a time? There was a time
          and it was of a sweet noise,
doutz brais e critz,
          for the woman who was Sophia
and for the parting, for *alba lux*,
          a parting worth a song —
meaning it meant something,
          a time, a year of meaning
and the light shimmered.
          Petals shimmered also on the tree
nearby the waters of Gihon,
          nearby the mountain of Golgotha.
But the name of the mountain is Whiteface,
          and the mill-dam washed out, Gihon
is loose, smashed in the longest winter.
          The mirror drips, the light is tarnished.
No one is here, is that clear —
          no one. The pronoun is you.
Whom will you forsake today?

Missing the Bo in the Henhouse

In here, caught by the storm. How the rain beats
on the metal roof! And hens peck at my feet,

these my ladies, their mournful pessimism, ayie,
ayie, ayo, and my boy whom I have loved — how

shall I say it or sing it? — more than myself,
more than my poems (that are myself),

more than the world (that is my poems),
ladies, these thirteen years, and now

he is turning, turning away. I know
we are "carried about the sun," about and about,

this conglomeration, a higgeldy-piggeldy
planet, incomprehensible, I could not

be part of it. And I am.
Carried. Desire long ago beaten out,

so that I wanted small things only, a song,
a boy. No, it will not cohere, this "world";

relentless the years and it will not. Mind
cannot make it. Ladies, do you know ever

what it means to be carried? Woe, ladies,
the boy is turning. A current runs on the grass.

And the dark falls early. Come now, up to your roost
and let the evening dance begin, the slow sarabande —

aft by fore, or aft by aft, which
shall it be? — turning, turning in the cadence

of your song. Ayie, ayie, ayo. Slower
and slower. Good night, ladies,

in your hurtling house. The time of the mouse
has come, the rain strums on your roof.

Keep close and keep warm. Bless me if you are able,
commend me to the storm. Good night, good night.

Aura

All day the mountain
flared in blue
September air.

The valley lay stunned
by color,
autumn's maple-brightness.

Now twilight comes;
not dark but a moment's
clarity, so that brute

wonder drains
from my eyes, relieved
by the evening star,

there, calm, over
the horizon, a lucidity,
a lucency. That light, far

lavender, restores
distance
and measure,

and inside my skull I rise
tall and free again.
Then

the mountain, free too
in its subduing,
intercedes, a new presence now,

a sense given beyond
color, around and surrounding —
is it shadow, is it

a blue myth coming to be?
Ah, wonder gone, how
lovely this welcoming! I see,

I see the new dimension, form
wavering into essence
and shimmering — oh,

so slightly! — back to
new form, while
the mountain looks at me.

Paragraphs

1

Begin right here. The Campground Road. Some calls it
    the
Hogback, but that's up higher. Down here's the river.
And there's Vermont, all ridge and valley
and all cockeyed — seem'z'o. Over
acrost is the hayth-o-land, Whiteface and all,
Madonna, Mansfield. Butternut's back here. And Baldy
Langdell's uncle's place was right there,
him that set his house as square
as his own square Yankee head afore he died   and Baldy
    died and old
Jimmy   and Hank Rago
King, Malcolm, Jackson and all —
    all in a breath of years.
                A cold wind,
                        old and cold,
sprung these waterdrops from a bare birch bough,
these lightdrops scattering to the edge
of a pool of darkness. Or say we could glimpse
    Vivaldi's parchment now,
his hand flinging down a bright arpeggio . . .

2

Keep going. *There's nothing else to do.* Past
the few farms remaining, Manchester's, Jones's.
Past brutishness new since last
I drove here, sliced stone,
eviscerated hills. And then the worst,
these superadded trailers, this prefab, damned fashion
out of Monterey or Bronxville, God knows where —

the national mean taking over. Or
the mean nationals.

                              Keep going, Waterville
to Johnson. I'd have thought
(almost) this was too tough, they couldn't spoil it,
ridge and riverbottom, massed heights,
granitic Vermont.   But they've walked on Kailas
         and thrown
town dirt on snow-bright Sati,
         they've exulted
before Kali.   They've put their feet on the moon.

3
Ithiel Falls, below the Nazarene campground. A name
clinging to its old place. The falls were blown out
in a WPA so-called work program,
1934 I think, to avert
another flood like '27 that had been true bedlam,
death-night all over Vermont. Icy water, the flame
in the lungs. God!
                              Yet the dynamite
was a fool's work, wasted. What
caused the flood was a jam in the fall's crest,
where the old covered bridges,
floating loose on high water, came to rest,
creating a dam. But then the new bridges

that replaced them were ironwork. Could *they* float?
Ah, Ithiel Falls, lovely cascading down ferny ledges,
and I never saw it.
                              Why were the falls blown out?

4

Why was the passenger pigeon exterminated?
                              Sometimes
I dream of those bridges; downriver on the flood,
shapes in dark water, awash and lumbering.
Why did the beatitude
who shot the last otter in Otter Creek come home
bragging? I dream how they yawed and stumbled,
how they wallowed almost but not quite like the huge
Jurassic animals caught in the deluge.
Why were the braves castrated, the stretched squaws
bayoneted up their vaginas?
Bridges are only bridges, that's all, bumping along,
      spandrel and truss,
post, brace, beam —
                  arks
of a minor people and a time too small for grief,
crunching, foundering, gone in the rain-drenched dark.
I grow old, my dreams are factual and brief.

5

Not night now. Dawn. Six o'clock, a November morning.
But raining still. I stop. In the blown falls the river
sinks on a long grade, curling
through the dogleg. I lower
my window. Rain hisses on the coarse snow remaining
from yesterday's freeze where broken stems of mullen
fence the ditch. A grove of popples,
grayish-green, is a drabness opposite,
with one stark white birch outstanding. A jay,
slanting tidily across the water
to a low branch, jeers as he goes. Way away,
way in the East, beyond our boarded up
Nazarenes, the sun struggles in a fog.

                                    Once at Walden
it was the "morning star" calling us to the order
of this world.
            Tell me   Henry David   are you still called?

6
The Lamoille River Valley otherwise known
as these objects jays trees snows that wont cohere
or where on the waters of darkness Apollyon
stalks to make this hour
dawn's awful madness in the Valley of Humiliation
and him the Angel of Death but Im no Christian
and first becomes last coherence fails
connections cherished 50 years and all's
lost no art more Ill write what I want how I want
dont bug me about my words
the vision is cold chaos and I need what warmth
my old mind knows I rub my beard
I crank my window closed but there there the Prince of
        Prose
Apollyon water-marcher his terrible swift regard
flinging look his icy pointed oldwords where he goes.

7
Arthritic gray snowlight hobbles down the valley
        westward.
It is day. Who also will choose my delusions and bring
my fears upon me? Engrafted words
I sing and sing and sing
upon blocky objects floating downriver, my days, while
        my godhood

ordains resolutions, a chaos of light, of flood,
a *catastrophe*. I turn the key, ram
the old truck in gear, and grind home
down the Campground Road toward the colorless, futile
dawn — past Farrell's,
up Stearn's Hill, past the Whiting Lot. More trailers,
earth crumbling and eroding visibly
beneath the snowcrust, pines and birches massacred. I
    feel
nothing but cold. I catch my reflection on the wet
    window, alone,
a face old and broken, hunched over Ixion's wheel.

*   *   *

8
the one called Next steps up
to the wall. a face detailed
and well remembered. but
my voice won't call
when i try it. stuck. i shut
my eyes. i hear the gunbolts
slide home. i open
my eyes. my hands
are missing. i reach.
i have nothing but wrists.
the face falls down. i retch.
the next one is called Next.
so dream after dream they keep
going. yet i'm sound awake.
the world has gone to sleep.

*   *   *

85

9

It was the custom of my tribe to be silent,
to think the song inwardly, tune and word
so beautiful they could be only held,
not sung; held and heard
in quietness while walking the end of the field
where birches make a grove, or standing by the rail
in back of the library in some northern
city, or in the long dream of a tower
of gothic stoniness; and always we were alone.
Yet sometimes two
heard it, two separately together. It could come
nearby in the shadow of a pine bough
on the snow, or high in the orchestral lights,
or maybe (this was our miracle) it would have no
intermediary—
                    a suddenness,
                              indivisible, unvoiced.

                    *   *   *

10

"There was this girl   18, 19   and slight
the way they are in that country   (you know)   laying
by the others in the ditch   taking
the bullets
with her body/   with which she shielded
as best she could   both her little child
and her zillion-year-old grandmother"
                              hic divisio
facta est inter Teutonicos et Latinos
Francos   circa 843 a.d./
                    or,
                    ahi serva Italia

di dolore ostello—
Dante who made it all ours and even more terrible
than perhaps it was   eloquence
so grave and so sweet.
                    "Her mouth was narrow
blood-choked/   we thought her eyes widened
more in incredulity than pain..."
                                        Ahi
            thou inn of sorrow.

                    *   *   *

11
Oh I loved you Pete Brown. And you were a brother
to me Joe Marsala. And you too sweet Billy Kyle.
You Sid Bechet. And Benny Carter.
And Joe Jones. Cozy Cole.
Cootie Williams. Dicky Wells. Al Hall. Ben Webster.
Matty Matlock. Lou McGarity. Mel Powell. Fats Waller.
Freddie Green. Rex Stewart. Wilbur & Sid
de Paris. Russ Procope. And Sister Ida
Cox dont forget her. And Omar Simeon. Joe Smith.
Zutty Singleton. Charlie Shavers.
Specs Powell. Red Norvo. Vic Dickenson. J.C.
        Higginbotham.
Nappy Lamare. Earl Hines. Buck Clayton.
Roy Eldridge, Pops Foster. Johnny Hodges. Ed Hall.
Art Tatum. Frankie Newton. Chu Berry. Billy Taylor.
And oh incomparable James P. Johnson.

                Brothers I loved you all.

                    *   *   *

12

I was watching the telly not serious you know just looking
with my wife there too and feeling all right after a dinner
at home together for once with our own cooking
and afterwards a whiskey for sipping
and I really was feeling all right   Almost shocking
when you consider my age (65) and my line of work
(political) but even in the Trouble
you forget sometimes/you have to   The doorbell
sounded/ Jenny bringing that big memo
to sign for the early pickup
I opened   It was a hooded man with a pistol
He fired three times/ there was a terrific
thud and I stood there watching a huge wall subside
under the pendulum stroke of a ball   while my wife's
     hysterics
drifted down the street like a shower of rain/
                     And then I died.

*   *   *

13

And the water/ the rising water
                           nothing like it
    for force
moving everywhere   embracing every obstacle
          as if it were love
             carrying everything before it/
                        a miracle
of conversion
              See how it spreads out & across
    the field
          making a nacreous sky-reflecting lake
        where geese

                    in thousands
rest for four days
                    on the long journey to Hudson's Bay
Rills rivulets streams springs ditches pools
                    it's a watery world
all trace of the old order going fast/
                              it spills
                    mud and the rich mould
              of its long astonishing suppuration
                                   and then
it's over
              all at once the movement has come full
and everyone
              puts on shirts of bright triumphant green.

                    *   *   *

14
In filthy Puerto Rico there lives a bird with no
legs and transparent wings, a somewhat small
bird whose flight is awkward and slow
yet it spends its whole
existence in flying. Luckily it knows how
to ride high currents above the eagles, hawks, crows
and all the preying host that seeks
its life continually. As long as it keeps
above them, soaring between them and the sun,
it cannot be seen, partly
because the predators are blinded by the exceeding
        shine
of brightness, partly because the heart
of the bird is the only thing that shows, a speck

in its transparency. High it flies, flies, flies, hungry and
    hurt,
until at last it falls forever on filthy Puerto Rico. And the
    name of the bird is blank.

*   *   *

15
''I am a fanatic lover of liberty, considering it
the unique condition in which intelligence, dignity,
and human happiness may develop and grow;
not the purely formal liberty
conceded, measured out, and regulated by the State,
an eternal lie which in reality represents
nothing more than the privilege
of some founded on the slavery
of the rest; not the individualistic, egotistic,
shabby and fictitious liberty
extolled by the school of J.-J. Rousseau and the other
schools of bourgeois liberalism,
which gives us the would-be rights of all men
as embodied in a State that limits the rights of each —
an idea which leads inevitably to the reduction

16
of the rights of each to zero. No, I mean the only
kind of liberty that is worthy of the name,
liberty that consists in the full development
of all the material, intellectual, and moral
powers which lie hidden in every person; liberty
which knows no restrictions beyond those
determined by the laws
of our individual natures,
which cannot properly be regarded as restrictions

since they are not imposed,
but are immanent and inherent, forming
the very basis of our material, intellectual,
and moral being — they do not limit us, they are
the real and immediate conditions of our freedom.''
— Thus living light cast back from a burnt-out star.

                        *   *   *

17
RAVAGE, *v.t.* To lay waste; to subject
to depredations; to work havoc or devastation upon;
to sack; plunder; despoil. *Syn.* —
RAVAGE, DEVASTATE, SACK
agree in the idea of despoiling or laying waste.
Ravage emphasizes the idea of violence: *devastate*,
that of waste or ruin; *sack*,
that of plunder or pillage. One *ravages*
or *devastates* a country, one *sacks* a town.

Unquote.

                        Please/
distinctions are important. There's still one man
who chooses with care. Anyone who agrees
may love me or not, but those condemning
my methods never will.

                        Regard the breeze
how it plucks bright autumn leaves
            one after another
                        to expose the timber.

91

18
And so with paragraphics.

                                      It was in summer
that lovely word chosen with care when I
first loved this valley where the river
was a curving ribbon of sky
lacing together the fields of every color
potatoes timothy mustard alfalfa clover
and purple widemarching corn. The farms
lay scattered in their places, a barn,
a house, fenced fields irregular. Their old
horse-drawn mowers
and manure spreaders rusted in the yards. Fold
within fold the darkening hills arose
toward glowing mountains. Here was a peacock, there
a Mongolian pheasant — no exotics, no more
than the useless horse or ox, for this was where

19
all things lay in nature, even the plastic flowers,
the flowering plastics,

                              the plastic farmers . . .

                                        Wordsworth!
thou should'st be living in this hour:
Vermont hath need of thee/
                                        Carruth
being at all events not up to it;
                                        the ancient power
of that vision is gone.
                        Gone? Was I bemused? The scars
are not new, the macadam was here then,
half the forests lay in slashed ruin,
the river's blue was more likely not sky

but the paintworks in Hardwick
cleaning its vats again. And yet
                              somehow
it *was* absorbed,   humanity sick
with greed, with loathing, somehow was taken in
by earth, water, mountain . . .

                              No more! The weak
have conquered and the valley is their domain,

20

ugly, evil, dying. The old soft lines,
knoll and glen, mountain and river, that held
the farms like poems curled in time,
have been ripped out,
                              raveled,
wrenched apart. The connections gone. It was dynamite
did it
        more than chainsaws or the great Cats, but —
                      ahi
                              it was men's minds
that did it!

              In this town, Johnson,
some have sold their own and everyone's
birthright to the ravagers, on our east and our west,
and particularly these two:
André Tournailler (*Anglice*, Toenailer) and Jacob Blesh.
Yes, townsmen, friends, I name *you,*
Andy and Jake, against every rule of Yankee decorum,
I name you in your public guilt. Here and now.
Look, the trailer park, filling station, plastic ranches,
        the rural

21

slums par excellence that were your farms! And all
for a hot pocketful of dollars.

                    I don't say others
haven't done as much, Farrells, Hills,
Berrys, Lahouillers, Parkers,
and so on — the length of the valley, to Hyde Park,
      Morrisville,
Wolcott, Hardwick, or westward to Lake Champlain,
a shambles, ravaged, devastated, gone,
or going fast.   All in the name
of "development." But good friends, where are your
      dollars
now? And who has profited?
Not farmers. Not (God knows) poets. None of us. The
      poor
play patsies again for mean-spirited
weaselly downcountry men, the capitalists, varmints
come ravaging in our dooryard like the strange coyotes
come from the west.

          And your *best* is what you gave them,
                       o my friends —
          your lives, your farms.

22

Now tell me if we don't need a revolution! Black
is the color of my only flag/

                    and of man's hope.
Will revolution bring the farms back?
Gone, gone. The only crop
this valley will grow now is the great landwrack,
breakage, erosion, garbage, trash, gimcrack.
We burn it. The stink trails in the air,
a long thin smoke of floating despair

down the time of our valley. Someday we will be free,
someday when it's too late.
It's true, the real revolutionary is one who can see
all dark ahead and behind, his fate
a need without a hope: *the will to resist.*
The State is universal, the Universe is a state.
Now ask me if I am really an anarchist.

*   *   *

23
Another hard, hard morning with a hard snow
Falling small and fast. It is eight below.
Yet the ash pail brims. I must go
Out to the garden and sow
This remnant of value where the beans will grow
Next summer maybe. The goddamned gods bestow
And men...
                    are at best a paradigm
Sowing and reaping in the void of time.
Or say that one must do what one does as though
It might mean something, so—
Broadcasting ashes, swinging my shovel low,
Spreading this color that I don't know,
Dirty lavender, dirty pearl, row upon row,
Death upon death, ''sowing the ashes,'' to and fro,
A *tour de force* in an abandoned studio.

*   *   *

24
And I was past caring   so many, too many men,
so many children/   body broken, slack
as the spirit   skin & bone
like a burlap sack

95

with a litre of rice in the bottom.

No one
wants lugging that around,

let the others run,
I said, and sat right down, there
where I was, and looked up into the air
to see it coming.

And when it came (that spout
of flaming jelly)   I cursed
and then I made a great sound: no shriek, no shout,
more like an enormous croak — the worst
I had ever heard.

For once then   *once*   I knew
what I had done was the most

and maybe the first
human thing I had ever been permitted to do.

*   *   *

25
Reading myself, old poems, their inside truth that was
(is, is!) crucial, tree stark in lightning glimpse, hidden
mostly by the storm: complexities,
modes, names, manners,   words laden
with terror. What true voice? Where? Humiliated, in
      throes
of vacillation, roundhead to cavalier to ivy league to
      smartass —
never who I was. Say it plain:
death/beauty, loneliness/love, wisdom/pain,
they the simple coordinates. Was it shameful
to be insane, or so grotesque
to wrench lucidity out of nowhere? Yet my call
came a whisper, my sentence an arabesque,

my song falsetto. Put the book back on the shelf.
Gone goodness. Dear mother, dead father, what
    burlesque
of feeling phonied us, that made you make me hate
    myself?

*   *   *

26
A day   very solid   February 12th, 1944
cheerless in New York City
                                (while I kneedeep
elsewhere in historical war
was wrecking Beauty's sleep
and her long dream)
                        a day (blank, gray) at four
in the afternoon, overheated in the W.O.R.
Recording Studios. Gum wrappers *and* dust
and a stale smell. A day. The cast
was Albert Ammons, Lips Page, Vic Dickenson,
Don Byas, Israel
Crosby, and Big Sid Catlett. (*And* it was Abe Linkhorn's
birthday.) And Milt Gabler
presided over the glass with a nod, a sign. Ammons
counted off
                a-waaaaan,,,   *tu*!

            and went feeling
his way on the keys gently,
                        while Catlett summoned

27
the exact beat from —
            say from the sounding depths, the universe . . .
When Dickenson came on it was all established,
no guessing, and he started with a blur
as usual, smears, brays — Christ

the dirtiest noise imaginable
                    belches, farts
                                curses
but it was music
                music now
                        with Ammons trilling in counterpoise.
Byas next, meditative, soft/
                        then Page
with that tone like the torn edge
of reality:
                and so the climax, long dying riffs —
groans, wild with pain —
and Crosby throbbing *and* Catlett riding stiff
yet it was music   music.
                        (Man, doan
fall in that bag,
                you caint describe it.)
                                Piano & drum,
Ammons & Catlett drove the others. *And* it was done
and they listened *and* heard themselves
                better than they were, for they had come

28
high above themselves. Above everything, flux, ooze,
loss, need, shame, improbability/   the awfulness
of gut-wrong,   sex-wrack,   horse & booze,
the whole goddamn mess,
And Gabler said "We'll press it"   *and* it was
        "Bottom Blues"
BOTTOM BLUES   five men knowing it well   blacks
        & jews
yet music, music   high
in the celebration of fear, strange joy
of pain: blown out, beaten out

                          a moment ecstatic
in the history
of creative mind *and* heart/   not singular, not the
      rarity
we think, but real and a glory
our human shining, shekinah . . .   Ah,
                  holy spirit, ninefold
I druther've bin a-settin there, supernumerary
cockroach i' th' corner, a-listenin, a-listenin,,,,,,,
            than be the Prazedint ov the Wuurld.

            *   *   *

NOTES

"Alba." The Gihon, recorded in *Genesis*, II, 13, as one of the four rivers of paradise, is also a river in Vermont. Rising in the town of Eden, it flows southward and joins the Lamoille at a place overlooked by Whiteface mountain.

Paragraphs. 2, Kailas (pron. kīlás), Tibetan range, paradise of Siva. 3, the flood of 1927 in northern New England was the worst in modern history in that region. Many hundreds of covered bridges, especially the bigger ones, were lost and never replaced. 5, popple: ancient local name for the quaking aspen. "Morning Star": *Walden*, the last sentence. 6, *Pilgrim's Progress*. 7, *Isaiah*, 66:4; *James*, 1:21. 10, My Lai; the "partition of Verdun," a.d. 843, a treaty establishing the division between what we now call Germany and France; and *Purgatorio*, VI, 76, the beginning of Dante's bitter animadversion on the ills of 14th-century Italy, in the famous Sordello canto. 14, told me by a Puerto Rican student. 15, 16, "La Commune de Paris et la Notion de l'Etat," Michel Bakounine, 1871. 26-28, thanks to Nat Hentoff, who sent me to Ralph Gleason, who sent me to Milton Gabler; as Mr. Gabler said: "Not a bad parlay." The original recording was Commodore No. 1516B.